Living in the
Sahara

Nicola Barber

Chicago, Illinois

Designed by Richard Parker and Manhattan Design
Printed and bound in China by SCPC

12 11 10 09 08
10 9 8 7 6 5 4 3 2

Library of Congress Cataloging-in-Publication Data
Barber, Nicola.
Living in the Sahara.
p. cm. -- (World cultures)
Includes bibliographical references and index.
ISBN-13: 978-1-4109-2816-0 (library binding-hardcover)
ISBN-10: 1-4109-2816-0 (library binding-hardcover)
ISBN-13: 978-1-4109-2825-2 (pbk.)
ISBN-10: 1-4109-2825-X (pbk.)
1. Tuaregs--Social life and customs--Juvenile literature. 2.
Sahara--Social life and customs--Juvenile literature.
I. Title. DT346.T7B37 2008
305.89'33--dc22
                    2007003285

Acknowledgments
The publishers would like to thank the following for
permission to reproduce photographs: Alamy Images/
David Poole p. **27**; Alamy Images/ Robert Estall Photo
Agency pp. **15, 21, 28**; Corbis Sygma/ Sophie Elbaz p. **9**;
Corbis pp. **8** (Frans Lemmens/Zefa), **13** (Ann Johansson),
16 (Martin Harvey), **19** (M. ou Me. Desjeux, Bernard),
23 (Laurent Gillieron/ EPA), **24** (Peter Adams/Zefa),
25 (Olivier Martel), **29** (Godong/ Philippe Lissac); Eye
Ubiquitous/ Hutchison p. **22**; Getty Images/ Photodisc
p. **26**; Lonely Planet Images/ Ariadne Van Zandbergen
p. **11**; Photographers Direct pp. **18** (Huib Blom), **20**
(Bruce Liron); Robert Harding Picture Library pp. **4**
(Sylvain Grandadam), **7** (Sergio Pitamitz); Still Pictures/
Frans Lemmens pp. **10, 14**; Still Pictures p. **12** (Jorgen
Schytte); Tips Images/ Mark Edward Smith p. **17**.

Illustrations by International Mapping.

Cover photograph of a Tuareg man in the Sahara
Desert, Timbuktu, Mali, reproduced with permission of
Photolibrary/ Ariadne Van Zandbergen.

The publishers would like to thank Karen Morrison for
her assistance with the preparation of this book.

Every effort has been made to contact copyright holders
of any material reproduced in this book. Any omissions
will be rectified in subsequent printings if notice is given
to the publishers.

Contents

Some words are printed in bold, **like this**. You can find out
what they mean on page 31.

Who Are the Tuareg?

The Tuareg live in the dry parts of northern Africa. They live in the Sahara Desert and **Sahel** region (see map on page 6). It is believed that the Tuareg are related to the **Berbers**. The Berbers were herders and farmers from North Africa.

▲ A group of Tuareg men gathers in the desert in Algeria.

WHERE DO THE TUAREG LIVE?

Today, the Tuareg are spread over Niger, Algeria, Mali, Burkina Faso, and Libya (see map opposite).

Traders

For centuries the Tuareg made their living from trading. They transported goods across the Sahara Desert. They traveled between North Africa and the rich cities to the southwest of the Sahara. The main goods were gold and salt. They carried them across the desert on camels. The Tuareg also kept herds of animals. Most Tuareg lived a mainly **nomadic** life. They moved from place to place with their animals. Many Tuareg became very wealthy from trade. They also made money from breeding and selling animals.

Today, many Tuareg are **seminomads**. They travel with their herds of animals for part of the year. At other times they return to their home area, where they grow crops. Other Tuareg have settled and live in one place all the time.

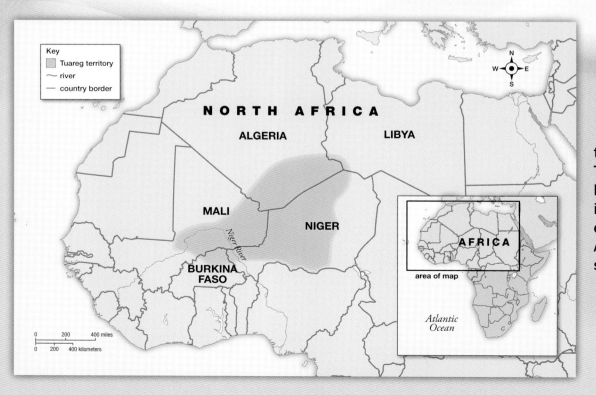

◀ In the 1960s, the traditional Tuareg desert lands were divided into the modern countries of North Africa that you can see on this map.

5

The Sahara Desert

The Sahara is the biggest desert in the world. It covers about 3.5 million square miles (9 million square kilometers). It is roughly the same size as the United States. The Sahara has a very hot, dry climate. There are less than 4 inches (10 centimeters) of rain every year. In some places it can rain twice in one week, but then it does not rain again for several years!

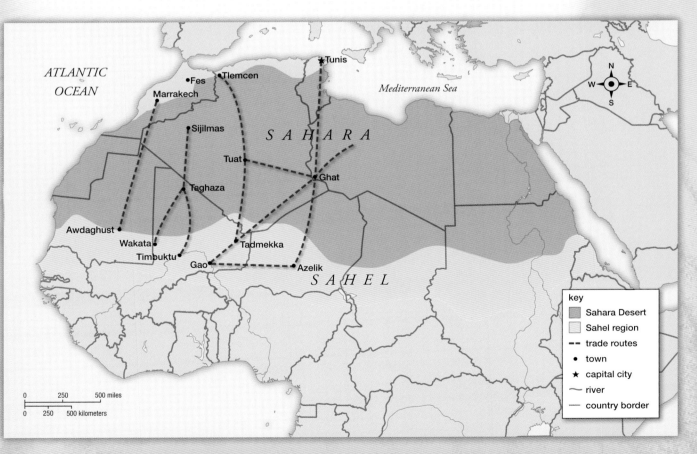

▲ The Tuareg live in the Sahara Desert and Sahel region. The Sahel region is the land between the Sahara Desert in the north and the more fertile region in the south.

▾ Very few plants and animals can survive in the Sahara Desert.

Harsh environment

In some places, the Sahara Desert is rocky and mountainous. In other places, it is all sand. The Tuareg have learned to live in the desert heat and to find water for their animals. They have also learned what clothes to wear and how to build suitable homes.

Today, **drought** and **famine** in the Sahara have forced many Tuareg to move to cities, south of the desert. This area is called the **Sahel**.

CAMELS

Camels are well suited to life in the hot desert climate. They store fat in their humps. The fat provides them with energy if food is hard to find. Camels have broad feet. These are ideal for walking on sand. Their eyes are protected from blowing sand by their long eyelashes.

Working in the Desert

Until the mid-1900s, the Tuareg's main work was transporting goods across the Sahara Desert. These goods included salt, gold, **ivory**, and **slaves**. Goods were carried by **camel caravans**. Camel caravans were made up of large numbers of camels traveling together. The caravans followed trade routes or paths (see map on page 6). They went from one **oasis** to the next.

An oasis is a place in the desert where there is a supply of water. At each oasis the camels were allowed to rest and were given food and water. Today, trucks take salt and fuel across the desert. There are very few roads. Camels are still used on some of the old routes.

▼ This oasis is in the Sahara Desert, in Libya. Plants and trees grow close to the water.

Farmers

The Tuareg have always kept herds of animals. These animals include goats, sheep, camels, and donkeys. At desert oases, there is water for raising crops. The Tuareg grow fruits and vegetables, such as dates, tomatoes, corn, and onions.

▲ A Tuareg man looks after his herd of goats in Mali.

SALT

Salt is important in the Sahara. People who live in hot climates lose a lot of salt as they sweat. They must eat enough salt to replace the salt they lose. Without salt, people can become very sick and even die. Salt is mined in the desert and carried across the desert by the Tuareg.

Desert Homes

Nomadic people have homes that can be easily put up or taken down. Many Tuareg families live in tents or huts. These homes can be carried from one place to another. Today, some Tuareg have settled in one place. They may live in houses that are made out of stone or mud brick.

▲ This traditional house in the Sahara in Algeria is made from mud.

▾ Tuareg men make tea next to a hut made from mats in Mali. You can see the wooden poles of the frame beneath the mats.

Tuareg tents and huts

A Tuareg tent has a covering made from goatskins. The goatskins are stretched over a frame. The frame is made from wooden poles. A Tuareg hut is made from mats. The mats are woven from grass or palm leaves and tied to an arched frame. The shape of the hut is like a boat turned upside-down. Some Tuareg also build cone-shaped huts. These huts are made from grass.

MAKING A TENT

Tuareg women sew goatskins into long strips. These strips are joined together to make a tent covering. Up to 40 skins are often used to cover a tent. A big tent for wealthy families might use many more skins.

Tuareg Life

In the past, Tuareg **society** was divided into five different classes. There were **nobles**, **vassals**, **slaves**, religious leaders, and artists or blacksmiths.

The nobles were wealthy Tuareg. They owned land and camels. They organized trade across the Sahara Desert. Vassals looked after the herds of animals. The Tuareg captured people to work for them as slaves. Religious leaders were holy men who followed the religion of **Islam**. They were called *marabouts*. Artists or blacksmiths made tools, saddles, and other equipment needed by the Tuareg.

◄ A Tuareg blacksmith works in a village in Niger.

▲ A newly married Tuareg couple share a tent in a village in Niger.

Marriage

Traditionally, the Tuareg married someone from their own class and were **nomadic**. Today, these traditions are disappearing, and the Tuareg are living more settled lives.

When a Tuareg woman gets married, her family makes a tent for her. In **rural** areas, the Tuareg still live in family **compounds**. Compounds are made up of several tents, which are named after the married woman. It is the Tuareg women who own the tents and everything inside them.

The diet of the Tuareg is based around milk. Milk comes from their camels and goats. The Tuareg also eat a **grain** called **millet**. They use the millet to make bread, or they make a kind of porridge. They also mix it with goat cheese, dates, and water to make a thick drink.

The Tuareg grow their own crops of fruits and vegetables at desert **oases**. They eat fish from the Niger River. They only eat meat—usually goat or camel—on special occasions. The Tuareg who live in towns or cities have a more varied diet.

◄ A Tuareg man tends his crops at an oasis.

DRINKING TEA

The Tuareg love drinking tea. They flavor it with sugar and often mint. The ceremony of making tea is very important. There are always three cups poured from a pot. The Tuareg say that the first cup is strong, like youth. The second is weaker and mild, like middle age. The third is sweet, like old age.

Clothes

It is important to protect bare skin from the hot desert sun. The Tuareg wear layers of loose-fitting clothes. The layers cover their bodies from head to toe. The cotton layers trap sweat. This helps to keep the body cool.

The Tuareg men wear a **turban** on their heads. The turban has a **veil**. The veil covers most of the face. The veil protects the face against sun and sand. It is also believed to keep away evil spirits. When a man is talking to someone important or someone older than himself, he pulls the veil high over his mouth and nose. This is a sign of respect.

▸ This man is wearing the traditional long robes and turban of the Tuareg. His veil is pulled down to show his face.

Men wear long robes. They have loose shirts and pants beneath. Women wear long skirts and blouses. After they have married, Tuareg women wear scarves to cover their hair. Today, in towns and cities, Tuareg clothing is more varied. Some wealthier people wear Western-style clothes, such as jeans and T-shirts.

◀ These Tuareg women in Libya wear long robes and scarves for protection from the hot sun.

THE "BLUE PEOPLE"

The Tuareg are often known as the "Blue People." Their turbans and veils were once made from cloth dyed blue with **indigo**. The dye often turned the Tuareg's skin blue. Today, they wear many different colors. Men's blue head coverings are often reserved for special occasions.

17

School and Learning

In the past, most Tuareg children did not go to school because Tuareg families moved from one place to another. Also, many Tuareg parents did not want their children to go to school. They believed that children should learn the skills needed for life in the desert. When the French took over the region, they tried to introduce schools for the Tuareg. But many Tuareg parents still refused to send their children to school.

▲ Children learn to read and write at a desert school near the Niger River.

◀ Children are being taught in French at this school for Tuareg **nomads** in Niger.

School today

Today, many more Tuareg children go to school. In some places there are traveling schools. These schools follow the children when they move. Some children go to school for half of the year. Then, they travel with their families for the other half.

TAMASHEQ

The Tuareg have their own language. It is called Tamasheq. They are also taught in French, which is the main language of the region.

Leisure and Crafts

In **rural** areas in the desert, Tuareg people entertain themselves. They sing, dance, and play games. Tuareg people who live in towns and cities can go to the movies or watch television, like other townspeople.

Crafts

Crafts have always been important in Tuareg life. Tuareg artists and blacksmiths are very skilled at working with metal. They make fine jewelry in silver. They also make swords, daggers, and decorations for saddles. They make fine saddles from leather as well.

▲ A Tuareg silversmith is at work. The Tuareg are famous for their fine silver jewelry.

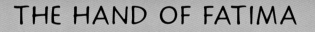

▶ This woman wears a traditional Tuareg necklace.

THE HAND OF FATIMA

Many Tuareg women wear special necklaces. The necklaces are decorated with five diamond shapes, joined together. The five shapes represent the five fingers of the hand of Fatima. Fatima was the daughter of the **Prophet Muhammad**. The Prophet Muhammad was the founder of **Islam**. The Tuareg follow the religion of Islam. Fatima had two sons, and the necklaces are powerful signs of **fertility**. They are also believed to protect the wearer from evil spirits.

Music and Poetry

Music and poetry are very important in Tuareg life. The music and poems are not written down. They are passed from woman to woman. Many Tuareg tales tell stories about African animals, such as hyenas, giraffes, or jackals.

◀ A Tuareg woman plays an *imzad*.

Traditional instruments

Women often play and sing music on special occasions, such as weddings and funerals. They play an instrument called an *imzad*, which is made from half a hollowed-out calabash. A calabash is a type of fruit. A goatskin is stretched over the hollowed-out calabash. The *imzad* has one string, which is made from goat hair and is played with a bow. The women may also play a small drum, which is made from goatskin. This drum is called a *tende*.

MODERN MUSIC

Tinariwen is a Tuareg band. The name "Tinariwen" means "empty places." The inspiration for the band's sound comes from traditional Tuareg music. The band also uses modern instruments, such as the electric guitar and drums.

◀ The Tuareg band Tinariwen performs in Switzerland in July 2006.

Celebrations and Ceremonies

The Tuareg are **Muslims** who follow the religion of **Islam**. However, the Tuareg have always mixed Muslim beliefs with their own traditional beliefs. They celebrate Islamic holy days, such as the birthday of the **Prophet Muhammad**. The Tuareg also celebrate national holidays, such as Niger Independence Day on August 3, that are not Muslim. Tuareg celebrations include music, feasts, and camel racing.

▲ These Tuareg men celebrate holidays with camel racing.

Ceremonies

Family celebrations are very important in Tuareg life. For example, when a Tuareg boy starts to wear his **veil**, at the age of about 18, there is a ceremony. A *marabout*, or holy man, performs the ceremony. Wearing the veil shows that the boy is old enough to marry. The celebrations for weddings often last for a week.

BABY NAMING

One week after a baby's birth, a special ceremony is held to name the baby. The baby is given a Tamasheq name as well as a name from the Islamic holy book, the Qu'ran.

- The name "Sahara" comes from *sahra,* an Arabic word meaning "desert."

- The Sahara has huge areas of windswept sand dunes. These dunes are called *ergs*.

- The average temperature in the Sahara during the summer can reach over 100°F (38°C).

- The highest temperature officially recorded anywhere in the world was in the Sahara. It was recorded in Libya in September 1922. The temperature was 136°F (58°C).

▶ Sand dunes, called *ergs*, are constantly blown by the wind.

▾ Goats graze (feed) on the slopes of the High Atlas Mountains in the north of the Sahara.

- Although they are in a hot desert, the tops of some high mountains in the Sahara are sometimes covered with snow.

- There are about 90 large **oases** in the Sahara.

- Thousands of years ago, the Sahara was much wetter than it is today.

- The Tuareg are not the only people who live in the Sahara. The desert is home to other people. These include the Moors and the Tubu.

Could You Live Like a Tuareg?

1. You need to travel across the desert.
   What are the best animals to choose?
   A   Horses
   B   Donkeys
   C   Camels

2. Why is salt so important in the desert?
   A   To make food taste good.
   B   To replace the salt lost as you sweat.
   C   To throw over your shoulder for good luck.

3. Some guests come to visit you at your tent.
   What drink do you offer?
   A   Tea
   B   Warm water
   C   Ice water

4. Traveling through the desert, how do you protect yourself from the hot sun?

A   Wear a bathing suit.
B   Sing a song.
C   Wear clothes that cover your body from head to toe.

5. Which two languages do you learn at a Tuareg school?

A   French
B   English
C   Tamasheq

Find Out for Yourself

Books to read

Chambers, Catherine, and N. Lapthorn. *Deserts* (*Mapping Earthforms* series). Chicago: Heinemann Library, 2007.

Morris, Neil. *Earth's Changing Deserts*. (*Landscapes and People* series). Chicago: Raintree, 2004.

Websites

www.pbs.org/wnet/africa/explore/sahara/sahara_overview_lo.html
A website that allows you to explore the Sahara and learn more about its peoples

http://tinariwen.calabashmusic.com/
Learn more about Tinariwen and listen to some of its music.

Glossary

Berber ancient people from northern Africa who speak the Berber language

camel caravan large number of camels traveling together to transport goods from one place to another

compound enclosed area of land with buildings in it

drought time when little or no rain falls

famine time when there is not enough to eat

fertility ability to reproduce

grain cereal plant, such as wheat, millet, or barley

indigo natural, blue dye that comes from the indigo plant

Islam describes people who are members of the Muslim faith, or things relating to the Muslim faith

ivory hard, white material obtained from the tusks of elephants

millet type of tall cereal grass

Muslim describes someone who follows the religion of Islam

noble in the past, wealthy Tuareg who owned land and camels and organized trade across the Sahara

nomadic describes a way of life in which people (nomads) move from place to place

oasis (more than one: **oases**) place in the desert where there is water at or near the surface

Prophet Muhammad founder of Islam. Believed by Muslims to be the last messenger of God.

rural describes the countryside rather than towns or cities

Sahel dry, semidesert region in northern Africa that lies immediately south of the Sahara

seminomad way of life in which people move from place to place at certain times of year. They search for grazing for their herds of animals.

slave someone who is owned by another person and forced to work for him or her

society people who live in a particular place

turban head covering worn by men, made from a long piece of cloth that is wound around the head

vassal in the past, people who looked after the Tuareg herds of animals

veil piece of cloth that often covers the face

Index